THE SOUTHEND
UNITED QUIZ BOOK

THE SOUTHEND UNITED QUIZ BOOK

COMPILED BY CHRIS COWLIN
& PETER MILES

FOREWORD BY FRANK DUDLEY

APEX PUBLISHING LTD

First published in 2007, Updated and reprinted in 2007 by
Apex Publishing Ltd
PO Box 7086, Clacton on Sea, Essex, CO15 5WN, England

www.apexpublishing.co.uk

British Library Cataloguing-in-Publication Data
A catalogue record for this book
is available from the British Library

ISBN 1-904444-91-1   978-1904444-91-6

Typeset in 10.5pt Chianti BdIt Win95BT

Cover Design: Andrew Macey

Printed and bound in Great Britain

This book is in no way officially associated with Southend United Football Club

Authors' Note:
Please can you contact ChrisCowlin@btconnect.com if you find any mistakes/errors in this book as we would like to put them right on any future reprints. We would also like to hear from Southend United fans who have enjoyed the test! Visit my website: **www.ChrisCowlin.com**

FOREWORD

I can always remember my early playing days. I played football as a youngster with the Air Training Corps and somebody must have seen me playing and arranged for me to have two or three games with Southend United reserves, which I did. I thought I played terribly but they must have seen some potential there because within a month they had asked me to sign as a professional.

That was in 1945 and I was on seven pounds a week, with another pound or two pounds if I played in the first team. I remember my first team debut clearly. It was at the old Southend greyhound track, 'the Stadium' as they called it. To my amazement, the manager Harry Warren called me in and announced, "I am playing you against Watford on Saturday" and, sure enough, he put me in the team.

I was very nervous, especially walking onto the field. Beside me was this old chap from Watford, who was about ten years older than me. He said, "I understand that this is your first game." And when I confirmed that it was, he responded, "Well, you see that grandstand over there?", pointing over to the stand, "If you come anywhere near me this afternoon I will kick you right over the top." As you can imagine, I thought, 'What have I let myself in for?'

Again, personally I thought I had played a terrible game that day, but after a while I started to score goals and from then on I never really looked back. I had a wonderful time at Southend and played with some great players and friends, but the best was the then captain Jimmy McAlinden, an Irish international and a very, very good player.

I later had a good career with Leeds, Southampton, Cardiff City and Brentford before returning to Southend and a lengthy spell working in local government. I remain a big Blues supporter and the club are very good to me, I have a permanent seat at Roots Hall which they allocate to me each year. I am so pleased to see them doing so well, and I know for a fact that the present manager knows a bit about football and I think he is the best thing that has happened to the club in years. It is a thrill for me to write the Foreword for this book and hope you will enjoy it! I am sure all Shrimpers fans will find the book very testing and it will also help to revive one or two memories I am sure. Up the Blues!

Best wishes

Best wishes

Frank Dudley

Frank Dudley
Southend United Football Club (1945-1949)

INTRODUCTION

On behalf of Peter and myself I would first of all like to thank Frank Dudley for writing the Foreword to this book. I am very grateful for his help on this project and was truly delighted when he agreed to write a few words. I would also like to thank the following people for writing some advanced reviews before publication: Dave Goody, Glenn Speller (BBC Essex), Shaun Peel (BBC Look East), Kevin Piper (Anglia TV) and Stephen Lee (Anglia TV), Derek Davis (East Anglian Daily Times), Tom King (Southend Echo), and four websites: www.4thegame.com, www.southendunited-mad.co.uk, www.ShrimperZone.com, www.sarfend.co.uk.

It was an honour to join forces with Peter Miles, who has an immense knowledge of Southend United Football Club and has co-written four other Shrimpers publications.

I would like to thank David Scriven at Southend United Football Club for his help and advice during the book's compilation.

I really hope you all enjoy this book. Hopefully it should bring back some wonderful memories!

Chris Cowlin.

Best wishes
Chris Cowlin

GOALSCORERS

1. Which Southend striker holds the record for the most goals in a season?

2. Who topped the Southend United goalscoring charts for three successive seasons during the 1950s?

3. Who holds the record for the fastest ever goal after the start of a game?

4. Which Southend striker has scored the most hat-tricks for the club?

5. What was unique about David Crown being Southend's leading goalscorer in the 1987/88 season?

6. What was unique about Southend's leading goalscorer in the 1921/22 season?

7. Who has scored the most career goals for Southend United?

8. Who is the only man to have scored a goal for Southend United at the old Wembley Stadium?

9. Who scored Southend United's first ever Football League goal?

10. Who is the only man to have scored in eight successive first team matches for the club?

WHO AM I?

11. I was born in Preston in 1954. I joined Southend United in July 1975 from Blackpool, scoring 31 times in 76 games before moving on to Chesterfield in February 1977.

12. I was born in Solihull and played for several clubs before first playing for Southend in the 1983/84 season. I then left for Exeter but returned to Roots Hall in August 1985. I scored 40 goals for the club but also collected seven red cards.

13. I am a striker who played 19 times for my country. I scored more than 250 career goals during a 19-year professional career.

14. I was born in New Addington and joined Southend for £40,000 in March 1988. No player has played more games for Southend in my position than me.

15. I started my career with Glenbuck Cherrypickers but went on to score 100 goals for Southend. I have a very famous footballing brother.

16. I played for Southend for ten seasons, making 419 appearances. I was Player of the Year in 1965/66. I now live in Kentville, Nova Scotia.

17. I joined Southend from Crystal Palace and scored 18 goals in my only season with the club. I was later capped by England.

18. I also joined Southend from Crystal Palace but took 290 games to score my three Southend goals. I was also later capped by England.

19. I scored 55 goals for Southend in 181 appearances. I also played for Grimsby, Sunderland, Chester and Swansea.

20. I was born in the West Midlands and played over 400 games for Southend. I was voted Player of the Year three times during my Southend career.

ROOTS HALL

21. Who was placed in charge of building Roots Hall?

22. What was the capacity of the old South Bank terrace?

23. Who was contracted to erect the steelwork for the East and North Stands?

24. When was the current South Stand built?

25. When did Southend return to Roots Hall?

26. In what year were floodlights erected at the ground?

27. How much did Roots Hall cost to build?

28. What game attracted the record crowd to Roots Hall?

29. The black seats in the East Stand previously saw service at another English football ground. Which one?

30. True or false: the ground is built on an ancient Roman burial site?

EARLY DAYS

31. Who chaired the initial meeting leading to the formation of the club?

32. Where did the meeting take place?

33. Who was engaged as the first Southend United manager/secretary?

34. Who was Southend United's first registered professional player?

35. Who was the club's first captain?

36. What was the club's first kit?

37. How many goals did Southend score in 65 games during 1906/07?

38. Why did Southend get into trouble for fielding Billy Leslie in four games during the 1908/09 season?

39. When Southend were denied promotion to the Southern League First Division for the 1907/08 season, who took their place?

40. Why were Southend nicknamed the "beef and mustards" during the 1910/11 season?

CUP TIES

41.   Who were the first top-flight club Southend defeated in a Cup match?

42.   Which was the first non-League club to defeat Southend at home in an FA Cup tie?

43.   What was unique about the first and second round FA Cup ties in the 1968/69 season?

44.   Which club were Southend playing in the FA Cup when the highest ever crowd for a Southend match of 53,043 gathered?

45.   When did Southend first reach the fifth round of the FA Cup?

46.   To whom did Southend lose their first ever major Cup final?

47.   Against whom did Southend play their first ever FA Cup tie?

48.   Who did Southend defeat 9-2 away from home in a 1946 FA Cup tie?

49.   What was unique about Southend's defeat of Swindon in a 2001 LDV Vans Trophy tie?

50.   Who scored a hat-trick in the 4-4 FA Cup second round draw with Northampton in December 1986?

MARK GOWER

51. In which year was Mark born in Edmonton - 1976, 1978 or 1980?

52. For which club did Mark play before joining Southend?

53. During 1999, which Scottish club did Mark spend time at whilst on loan?

54. At which North London club was Mark a trainee?

55. Which squad number did Mark wear during 2006/07?

56. Against which East Anglian side did Mark score in a 2-0 away win during March 2007?

57. Following on from the previous question, can you name the other Southend goalscorer?

58. How many League goals did Mark score for Southend during 2005/06?

59. Against which team did Mark score a last-minute equaliser to make the score 3-3 at Roots Hall in September 2006?

60. Which London team did Southend beat 5-0 with Mark scoring one of the goals during Febraury 2007?

SOUTHEND MANAGERS

MATCH UP THE MANAGER WITH THE PERIOD
HE MANAGED THE CLUB

61.	Bobby Moore	2003
62.	Ronnie Whelan	2003
63.	Alan Little	1921-1934
64.	Stewart Robson	1993-1995
65.	Ted Fenton	1993
66.	Dave Smith	1995-1997
67.	Barry Fry	1984-1986
68.	Peter Taylor	1961-1965
69.	Steve Wignall	1976-1983
70.	Ted Birnie	1999-2000

NATIONALITIES

MATCH UP THE PLAYER WITH HIS NATIONALITY

71.	Efe Sodje	English
72.	Spencer Prior	Scottish
73.	Jamal Campbell-Ryce	Republic of Ireland
74.	Franck Moussa	English
75.	Steven Hammell	Republic of Ireland
76.	Lee Bradbury	Nigerian
77.	Kevin Maher	Jamaican
78.	Alan McCormack	Belgian
79.	Richie Foran	English
80.	Stan Collymore	Republic of Ireland

SOUTHEND GOALKEEPERS

81. Which Southend goalkeeper played in the LDV Vans Trophy final in 2004?

82. Can you name the two goalkeepers that were used during 1998/99?

83. Which goalkeeper did Southend buy in June 2006 from Yeovil Town?

84. Can you name the two goalkeepers that were used during 2005/06?

85. Which goalkeeper spent three months on loan at Southend during 2000 and played 17 League games for Southend?

86. Which goalkeeper played 11 League games for Southend between 2001 and 2003?

87. How many League games did Neville Southall play for Southend in his career - 9, 19 or 119?

88. Which goalkeeper orginally came to Roots Hall on loan in 1974 but then went on to make nearly 250 appearances for the club?

89. Which team did Eric Steele join when he left Roots Hall in August 1988?

90. Which goalkeeper was given the squad number 30 during 2006/07?

2006/07

91. Which team did Southend beat 1-0 on the opening day of the season at Roots Hall?

92. Following on from the previous question, who scored the goal?

93. Which player scored a brace in the 3-1 home win in August 2006 against Sunderland?

94. Who managed Southend United during this season?

95. Against which top-flight team did Freddy Eastwood score in the League Cup fourth round 1-0 home win?

96. In December 2006, which two players scored the goals in the 2-1 win against Southampton at Roots Hall?

97. Which Midlands team did Southend beat 3-1 on New Year's Day?

98. Which player scored the goal against Leeds United in the 1-1 home draw?

99. Who was Southend chairman during this season?

100. Which London team knocked Southend out of the League Cup in the quarter-final?

APPEARANCES

101. Which Southend player has played the most first team games for the club?

102. Which Southend player has made the most League appearances for the club?

103. Which Southend player has played the most FA Cup ties for the club?

104. Which Southend player has played the most League Cup ties for the club?

105. Which Southend player has made the most substitute appearances in the first team?

106. Which Southend player made 230 consecutive first team appearances during the 1950s?

107. Which Southend player made 155 consecutive first team appearances between May 1989 and March 1992?

108. Which player has made the most substitute appearances for the first team without ever starting a match?

109. In the 1980/81 championship winning season, which three players played all 49 games in that campaign?

110. In the 1986/87 promotion season, which three players played all 56 games in that campaign?

AGES

111. Who is Southend's oldest post-war debutant at 39 years and 143 days?

112. Who is the only other 39-year-old post-war debutant?

113. Who is the youngest player to have made a first team debut at the age of 16 years and 76 days?

114. Southend last fielded a 16-year-old player in 2006. Who was he?

115. Who was 35 years and 169 days old when he first pulled on a Southend shirt in August 2005?

116. Who was 36 years and 174 days old when he scored his only Southend goal in March 1986 against Northampton Town?

117. Who was 40 years and 204 days old when he made his final appearance for Southend in November 1999 against Brighton and Hove Albion?

118. Who at the age of 16 years and 226 days is the club's youngest first team goalscorer?

119. During the year 1998, Southend had two debutants over the age of 34. Name both.

120. Which ex-England international was 33 years and 245 days old when he made his debut for Southend in January 1984?

ATTENDANCES

121. What is the largest home attendance for a Southend United League match?

122. Which cup tie attracted an attendance of 441 in November 1993?

123. During which season did Southend attract their highest aggregate attendance for 23 home matches of 258,267 spectators?

124. During which season did Southend attract their lowest aggregate attendance for 23 home matches of 44,364 spectators?

125. What is the lowest home crowd for a Southend first team fixture?

126. What is the lowest home crowd for a League fixture?

127. Which game attracted the largest home gate of the 2004/05 season?

128. What is the lowest away attendance recorded for a Southend League fixture?

129. What is the highest away attendance recorded for a Southend League fixture?

130. Which LDV Trophy final featuring Southend attracted the largest crowd?

INTERNATIONALS

131. Who was the first Southend player to gain an international cap whilst at the club?

132. Which future Southend player played against England in the 2002 World Cup?

133. Against whom did Tesfaye Bramble play his only international for Montserrat in 2005?

134. Which played won the most international caps whilst playing for Southend?

135. Which Southend player played for his country against Liechtenstein in June 1995?

136. Only two Southend players have scored at international level. Name them.

137. Three post-war Southend players have been capped by Northern Ireland. Who are they?

138. Only four Southend players went on to be capped by England at full international level after they left the club. Who are they?

139. When Ireland played Norway in October and November 1937, two Southend players were in their line-up. Name them.

140. Which player with six full Irish caps played for Southend during 2003?

GROUNDS

*DURING THEIR HISTORY SOUTHEND UNITED HAVE
PLAYED MATCHES ON THESE GROUNDS. WHO WOULD
THEY HAVE BEEN PLAYING?*

141. Lower Mead

142. Kingfield

143. Borough Park

144. Cassio Road

145. Windmill Ground

146. Holker Street

147. Green Pond Road

148. Browns Lane

149. Park Royal

150. White City

MATCH THE YEAR

MATCH UP THE EVENT WITH THE YEAR
IN WHICH IT TOOK PLACE

151.	League One champions	1992
152.	League Two play-off winners	1981
153.	Division Four runners-up	2006
154.	LDV Vans Trophy runners-up	1991
155.	Highest attendance of 31,033 against Liverpool in the FA Cup	2005
156.	Division Three runners-up	2005
157.	Division Four runners-up	2004
158.	LDV Vans Trophy runners-up	1972
159.	Stan Collymore signs for Southend	1979
160.	Division Four champions	1978

WHAT WAS THE SCORE? - 1

MATCH UP THE FIXTURE WITH THE FINAL SCORE

161. *3 November 1979*
     Carlisle United (A), Division Three   **1-7**

162. *29 April 1952*
     Ipswich Town (H), Division Three South   **7-0**

163. *21 November 1970*
     Weymouth (H), FA Cup   **4-0**

164. *12 September 1962*
     Shrewsbury Town (A), Division Three   **4-0**

165. *2 September 1974*
     Halifax Town (H), Division Three   **7-1**

166. *24 November 1951*
     Bournemouth & BA (H), FA Cup   **0-4**

167. *22 February 1975*
     Wrexham (A), Division Three   **7-0**

168. *13 October 1951*
     Aldershot (H), Division Three South   **6-1**

169. *29 March 1968*
     Workington (H), Division Four   **5-0**

170. *17 February 1976*
     Brighton & Hove Albion (H), Division Three   **0-6**

DIVISION 3 RUNNERS-UP 1991

171. Which player was Southend Player of the Year?

172. Who was the Southend manager during this season?

173. Who was top scorer with 26 goals (in all competitions)?

174. How many of their 46 League games did Southend win?

175. Against which team did Southend play on the opening day of the season, winning 2-1?

176. Which team won the Division Three title, beating Southend by 1 point?

177. Which team beat Southend 1-0 on the final day of the season?

178. During September 1990, which forward scored a brace in a 4-1 away win against Cambridge United?

179. Against which team did Southend record their biggest League home crowd?

180. How many clean sheets did Southend keep (in all competitons) - 10, 14 or 18?

CHRIS POWELL

181. From which team did Southend sign Chris in 1990?

182. In which position did Chris play for Southend?

183. In October 1990, against which team did Chris score at home in a 2-1 win?

184. Which manager signed Chris for Southend?

185. How many England caps did Chris win for his country - 5, 15 or 25?

186. Which ex-Liverpool player was manager of Southend when Chris left Roots Hall?

187. For which Premier League team did Chris sign in June 2006?

188. For which London club did Chris play between 1998 and 2004?

189. Against which team did Chris score in a 2-2 away draw in October 1992?

190. When Chris left Roots Hall in 1996, which club did he join?

TONY BENTLEY

191. In what position did Tony play for Southend?

192. In Tony's testiominal match in 1972, which team did Southend United play?

193. How many appearances (in all competitions) did Tony make for Southend - 319, 419 or 519?

194. In which season at Roots Hall was Tony awarded Player of the Year?

195. How many goals (in all competitions) did Tony score for Southend United - 7, 17 or 27?

196. In what year was Tony born - 1929, 1939 or 1949?

197. Which manager signed Tony for Southend United?

198. In November 1965 in the FA Cup first round Tony scored in the 3-1 win against which team?

199. In February 1966 in Division Three Southend United beat which team 5-3 at home with Tony scoring?

200. In January 1967 Tony scored agaisnt Hartlepool United in the 2-1 away win. Which player scored the other goal?

MANAGERS

201. Who was Southend's manager when they entered the Football League in 1920?

202. Who was appointed caretaker manager for one game in between the managerial reigns of Alvin Martin and Alan Little?

203. Who succeeded Dave Webb after his third spell in charge of the club ended in October 2001?

204. Which Southend manager holds the Football League record for goals scored in a career with a mammoth 434?

205. Which caretaker manager was in charge of the team for three games prior to the appointment of Steve Wignall?

206. Which Southend chairman acted as team manager in two separate spells during the 1960s?

207. Name the six Southend managers that won at least one full England cap as a player?

208. Which popular Southend manager was born in Dundee in 1933?

209. Who was in charge of Southend for their first ever League Cup tie in October 1960?

210. Which former Southend manager was born in Croydon in 1944?

EXOTIC FRIENDLIES

*SOUTHEND HAVE PLAYED A NUMBER OF FRIENDLIES ABROAD
OVER THE YEARS. WHICH COUNTRY WOULD THEY HAVE BEEN
IN WHEN THEY TOOK ON THE FOLLOWING CLUBS?*

211.   Angers FC (1953)

212.   Racing Club Malines (1953)

213.   Floriana (1955)

214.   Catania (1955)

215.   Saarbrucken (1957)

216.   Karlova Vary (1957)

217.   Groningen (1958)

218.   Hambourn (1958)

219.   Tula Metalist (1971)

220.   FC Volendam (1973)

TRANSFERS OUT

221. Who did Southend sell to Birmingham City for £800,000 in December 1994?

222. Who commanded a £500,000 fee when he moved to Everton in January 1994?

223. Tottenham paid £375,000 for which Southend player in June 1992?

224. Which Southend striker was sold to Nottingham Forest for £250,000 in March 1994?

225. Stoke City paid £200,000 for which Southend player in March 1997?

226. Which Southend player joined Blackpool for the curious fee of £111,111 in December 1979?

227. Which Southend player commanded a £120,000 fee when joining Crystal Palace in October 1973?

228. York City paid £100,000 for which Southend player in July 1999?

229. Which Southend player joined Stockport County for £50,000 in March 2001?

230. Who commanded a £40,000 fee when joining Aston Villa in June 1969?

TRANFERS IN

231. Which player joined Southend for £400,000 from Plymouth Argyle in July 1993?

232. In February 1996, which player joined Southend for £150,000 plus Dave Regis?

233. Who earned his club a £250,000 fee when joining Southend in July 1994?

234. £175,000 was spent on which Brentford player in October 1991?

235. Which international defender joined the club for £150,000 in July 1995?

236. Which Leyton Orient player cost £100,000 in July 1993?

237. Also in July 1993, a further £100,000 was spent on a player who would only start 12 games for the club. Name him.

238. In February 1980, a fee of £80,000 was given to Watford for the services of which player?

239. Boston United received £60,000 for which player in February 2001?

240. Which player cost £50,000 in November 1994 but would only make four substitute appearances before having his contract terminated?

HAT-TRICKS

241. Which two players scored hat-tricks in the 10-1 defeat of Aldershot in November 1990?

242. Which player scored a hat-trick of headers against Boston United in December 2002?

243. Only two Southend players registered Football League hat-tricks during the 1990s. Name them.

244. Who scored four goals against Orient in August 1985 in what was his first full appearance for the club?

245. Billy Best scored the most career hat-tricks for the club with nine, but which two players are equal second with seven each?

246. How many hat-tricks did Peter Silvester score for the club?

247. Who scored a hat-trick in the 7-0 defeat of Torquay United in February 1991?

248. In his first two seasons with Southend, how many hat-tricks did Freddy Eastwood score?

249. Who scored all four goals against Torquay United in September 1977?

250. Which two clubs have had the misfortune to be on the receiving end of five hat-tricks scored by Southend players since 1920?

SIMON ROYCE

251. From which club did Southend sign Simon in 1991?

252. In what position did Simon play for Southend?

253. For which London team did Simon sign when he left Roots Hall in 1998?

254. In what year was Simon born - 1961, 1971 or 1981?

255. What nationality is Simon?

256. Which manager brought Simon to Southend and handed him his debut?

257. Which manager was in charge when Simon left the club?

258. Which team did Simon play for between 2000 and 2003?

259. How much did Southend United pay for Simon in 1991?

260. During February 2007, for which London side was Simon playing when Southend won 5-0 at Roots Hall?

DAVID CROWN

261. In what position did David play for Southend?

262. From which club did David sign in November 1987?

263. How many League games did David play for Southend -
      113, 123 or 133?

264. Which manager signed David for Southend?

265. How many League goals did David score for the
      Shrimpers - 41, 61 or 81?

266. In November 1987 David scored his first Southend goal
      against which club in a 3-0 away win?

267. True or false: David won Southend Player of the Year in
      his first season at Roots Hall?

268. In April 1989 David scored a brace in a 2-1 home win,
      against which team?

269. When David left Roots Hall which team did he join?

270. In January 1990, against which team did David score a
      hat-trick in Division Four in a 5-0 home win?

FREDDY EASTWOOD

271. In what year was Freddy born - 1981, 1982 or 1983?

272. From which club did Southend sign Freddy?

273. During October and November 2004, Freddy was loaned to Southend and he made five appearances for the club, scoring how many goals - 0, 3 or 6?

274. How many goals did Freddy score for Southend during 2004/05?

275. In August 2005, against which side did Freddy score in a 1-1 home draw and then later in the game got sent off - Huddersfield Town, Brentford or Colchester United?

276. Freddy scored two hat-tricks for Southend during 2005/06, against which sides?

277. Against which club did Freddy score his first Southend hat-trick in 2004 in a 4-2 home win - Bury, Leyton Orient or Swansea City?

278. In March 2006 Freddy scored against Colchester United in a 3-0 away win. Which other players scored?

279. In what season did Freddy first win Southend Player of the Year - 2004/05, 2005/06 or 2006/07?

280. Which manager brought Freddy to Southend?

BILLY BEST

281. From which club did Billy sign to join Southend in 1968?

282. How many times did Billy win Southend United Player of the Year in his five seasons at the club?

283. Against which team did Billy score his first goal for Southend in a 2-2 draw in February 1968?

284. Which manager brought Billy to Southend?

285. How many hat-tricks (in all competitions) did Billy score for Southend in his career?

286. True or false: During 1968/69 Bill scored during the first, second, third and fourth rounds of the FA Cup?

287. In what month during the 1969/70 season did Billy score his first hat-trick of the season?

288. In April 1969 Billy scored a hat-trick against which team in Division 4 at home in a 4-2 win?

289. How many goals did Billy score during 1970/71 (in all competitions) for Southend United - 18, 20 or 22?

290. True or false: During December 1968 Billy scored five goals in a 10-1 home FA Cup second round win against Brentwood Town?

ALAN MOODY

291.   What record does Alan currently hold at Southend United?

292.   In what year was Alan born - 1950, 1951 or 1952?

293.   How many League appearances did Alan make for Southend United - 446, 546 or 646?

294.   How many League goals did Alan score in his Southend career - 21, 41 or 61?

295.   In what position did Alan play for Southend?

296.   When Alan left Roots Hall, which club did he join?

297.   Which manager gave Alan his Southend debut?

298.   Under how many managers did Alan play whilst at Roots Hall?

299.   What was special for Alan at the end of the 1974/75 season?

300.   Against which London team did Alan play for Southend in his testimonial in 1984?

GOALSCORING DEBUTS

301. Who scored twice on his Southend debut against Cheltenham Town in August 2003?

302. Who scored on his debut against Walsall in August 2005?

303. Which player found the net on his first Southend outing against Cambridge United in February 2004?

304. Who scored twice on his debut against Bury in August 1987?

305. Who scored twice on his debut against Notts County in November 1992?

306. Who scored in his only Southend appearance in January 1995?

307. Against whom did David Lee mark his Southend debut with a goal on the opening day of the 2000/01 campaign?

308. Who is the odd man out from these Southend strikers: David Whyte, Steve Phillips, Greg Shepherd and Neil Tolson?

309. Which two players scored on their Southend debuts against Millwall in August 1993?

310. Who scored on his debut against Crewe Alexandra in October 1986?

STAN COLLYMORE

311. In which Staffordshire town was Stan born?

312. From which non-League club did Steve Coppell sign Stan for Crystal Palace?

313. Against whom did Stan score two FA Cup goals for Southend in January 1993?

314. Apart from Southend, can you name the two clubs Stan scored for on his debut?

315. Against which country did Stan make his England debut at full international level?

316. Who was Nottingham Forest's manager when Stan left Southend in July 1993?

317. Which manager signed Stan for Liverpool for £8.5 million in July 1995?

318. What was the name of Stan's autobiography?

319. What was the name of the training camp Stan was at with Leicester City when the widely reported fire extinguisher incident occurred?

320. How many games did Stan play for his last club Real Oviedo?

BARRY FRY

321. Barry signed initially as an amateur for Manchester United in 1960. What career did he have to supplement his wages at the time?

322. Which club did Barry join after leaving Old Trafford?

323. Following on from the previous question, Barry was then a player at which London club, where he gained his first experience as a trainer?

324. With which club did Barry win the Southern League Division One title in 1970?

325. Which world-famous player did Barry sign for Dunstable Town when he was player/manager there?

326. What was the name of Barry's controversial chairman at Barnet?

327. What were the names of Barry's assistant manager and player/coach at Southend?

328. What was the score in Barry's first return to Roots Hall as manager of Birmingham City?

329. Following on from the previous question, can you name the six Southend players Barry subsequently signed for Birmingham City?

330. Can you name the Peterborough chairman from whom Barry bought controlling interest of the club in 2002?

SHAUN GOATER

331. Shaun was born in the capital city of Bermuda, which is?

332. Shaun is actually his middle name. What is his forename?

333. With which Bermudan club did Shaun make his name: Somerset, North Village or St George's?

334. Which English club offered Shaun a trial and subsequently a professional contract in 1989?

335. For which club did Shaun make his English League debut in October 1989?

336. Which club spent £175,000 on Shaun in July 1996?

337. Who was Manchester City manager when they signed Shaun for £400,000 in March 1998?

338. Against whom did Shaun score his 100th goal for Manchester City?

339. During Shaun's spell at Reading, at which club did he spend a month on loan in March 2005?

340. Shaun scored two braces for Southend in 2005, against which clubs?

RED CARDS

341. Name the three Southend players sent off against Swansea City in September 1998?

342. Name the three Southend players sent off against Swansea City in December 2003?

343. In August 2001, two Southend players were given the red card in a League Cup tie at Birmingham City. Name them.

344. Up to the end of the 2006/07 season, how many red cards had Kevin Maher collected for Southend?

345. Who owns the record for the most career red cards for Southend with seven?

346. In which season did Southend collect a record nine dismissals?

347. In December 1993 three players were sent off in a match at Roots Hall against Charlton Athletic. Phil Chapple and Colin Walsh were dismissed for the visitors, but who joined them for an early bath from Southend?

348. How many times was Paul Sansome sent off for Southend?

349. Southend had two players sent off at home to Exeter City in March 1999. Name them.

350. Which player was sent off three times in his first 17 matches for Southend between March and August 2001?

RICKY OTTO

351. In which year did Ricky sign for Southend?

352. How many League goals did Ricky score in his Southend career - 17, 27 or 37?

353. Which Shrimpers manager brought Ricky to Southend?

354. When Ricky left Southend in December 1994, which Midlands team did he join?

355. How much money did Southend receive for Ricky when he left Roots Hall?

356. In what year was Ricky born - 1957, 1967 or 1977?

357. True or false: Ricky's nationality is Scottish?

358. From which London team did Southend buy Ricky, having played for them between 1990 and 1993?

359. In what position did Ricky play for Southend United?

360. Who was Southend manager when Ricky was sold in December 1994?

ROY McDONOUGH

361. In what position did Roy play during his playing days?

362. How many spells did Roy have at Roots Hall - 1, 2 or 3?

363. In what year did Roy make his debut for Southend?

364. How many League goals did Roy score in his Southend career - 18, 38 or 58?

365. In what year was Roy born - 1950, 1954 or 1958?

366. In 1980, which Essex side did Roy join from Chelsea?

367. Roy scored his first Southend goal in a 4-1 away defeat, against which side?

368. In October 1983 Roy scored in a 3-0 home win against Leyton Orient. Which two players scored the other goals?

369. What nationality is Roy?

370. How many red cards did Roy receive whilst a Southend player - 5, 7 or 9?

POSITIONS IN THE LEAGUE

MATCH UP THE SEASON WITH THE POSITION IN
WHICH SOUTHEND FINISHED IN THE LEAGUE

371.	1991/92	15th in Division One
372.	2005/06	14th in Division Three
373.	1996/97	1st in League One
374.	1987/88	12th in Division Two
375.	2002/03	11th in Division Three
376.	1979/80	17th in Division Three
377.	1963/64	22nd in Division Three
378.	1993/94	19th in Division Three (South)
379.	2000/01	17th in Division Three
380.	1926/27	24th in Division One

POT LUCK

381. Who managed Southend from 1965 until 1967?

382. From which team did Southend sign Lewis Hunt in July 2004?

383. In what year was the club formed - 1906, 1907 or 1908?

384. How much money did Southend receive from Nottingham Forest for Stan Collymore in 1993?

385. Can you name all three of the club's nicknames?

386. In what year did Southend move to Roots Hall?

387. From which team did Southend sign Jamal Campbell-Ryce in 2006?

388. True or false: Southend United were once top of Division One for three hours on News Year's Day in 1992?

389. What is Stan Collymore's middle name?

390. True or false: In September 1991 Southend missed seven penalties in succession?

LDV VANS TROPHY
RUNNERS-UP 2004

391. Which manager was in charge of Southend during this Cup run?

392. Which team did Southend beat 2-1 in the first round at home?

393. Following on from the previous question, can you name Southend's scorers in the game?

394. Southend United beat Swansea City in the second round away from home. What was the score?

395. Which club did Southend beat 3-0 in the third round?

396. Which London team did Southend beat 4-0 in the semi-final?

397. Which team did Southend play in the Southern final?

398. Following on from the previous question, what was the aggreate score in the Southern final over the two legs?

399. Southend lost in the final to Blackpool. Can you name seven of the starting eleven players?

400. Following on from the previous question, at what stadium was the game played?

BITS AND PIECES

401. By the end of the 2006/07 season, Southend had never played a competitive fixture against only one English League club. Name them?

402. What occurred in the matches at The Kursaal against Newport (September 1923) and Brentford (March 1932)?

403. Why was the match abandoned at Northampton Town's County Ground in August 1980?

404. At which "home" ground did Southend play matches during World War Two?

405. From what kidney disease did legendary Southend goalkeeper Charlie Cotton die at the age of 30 in 1910?

406. In which two years did Roots Hall stage England amateur international matches against Scotland?

407. Who was the first Southend substitute used in a game in August 1965?

408. What was the name of the Rugby League club that shared Roots Hall in the 1984/85 season?

409. For wha misdemeanour were Southend players Joe Wilson, Dave Robinson and Bertram Jones taken to court in September 1932?

410. In the infamous 4-3 FA Cup win over Chesterfield in January 1939, for what offence was Alf Smirk booked by the referee?

OVERSEAS PLAYERS

CAN YOU MATCH THE EXOTIC BIRTHPLACE TO THE CORRECT SOUTHEND UNITED PLAYER?

411.	Cape Town, South Africa	Lars Unger
412.	Arnheim, Holland	Franck Moussa
413.	Redondo Beach, United States	Dominic Iorfa
414.	Montreal, Canada	Eddie Firmani
415.	Brignoles, France	Sada N'Diaye
416.	Brussels, Belgium	Jeroen Boere
417.	Lillehammer, Norway	Errol Crossan
418.	Dakar, Senegal	Mike Lapper
419.	Eutin, Germany	Regis Coulbault
420.	Lagos, Nigeria	Pettar Belsvik

PLAYER OF THE YEAR

CAN YOU NAME THE PLAYER AWARDED SOUTHEND PLAYER OF THE YEAR IN THE FOLLOWING SEASONS?

421.   *1978/79, 1979/80 and 1982/83 (a midfielder)*

422.   *1967/68, 1969/70 (a forward)*

423.   *1974/75 (a defender)*

424.   *1980/81 (a forward)*

425.   *1983/84 (a defender)*

426.   *1987/88 (a midfielder)*

427.   *1988/89 (a forward)*

428.   *1994/95 (a goalkeeper)*

429.   *1996/97 (a defender)*

430.   *2000/01 (a midfielder)*

NON-LEAGUE FA CUP TIES

MATCH THE CORRECT YEAR WITH EACH
OF THE FOLLOWING FA CUP RESULTS

431.	Trowbridge Town 0, Southend United 2	1927
432.	Ilford 0, Southend United 2	1933
433.	London Paper Mills 0, Southend United 1	1937
434.	Brush Sports 1, Southend United 6	1953
435.	Southend United 7, Weymouth 0	1946
436.	Southend United 4, Automotive Products Leamington 0	1957
437.	Southend United 1, Wellington Town 0	1959
438.	Finchley 1, Southend United 3	1970
439.	Southend United 6, Oswestry Town 0	1974
440.	Walthamstow Avenue 0, Southend United 1	1977

BIRTHPLACES

441.   Out of Southend's 858 players used since 1920, how many were actually born in Southend - 12, 18, 24, 29 or 31?

442.   What do former Southend players Jimmy Stevenson, Lawrie Kelly, Mark McNally and Alex Burns all have in common?

443.   Southend had four post World War Two players that were born in Belfast. Can you name them?

444.   What do Ricky Otto, Leon Constantine, Jim Corbett and Mel Capleton have in common?

445.   Name the only Southend player born in the Isle of Wight.

446.   What do Eric Steele, Taffy Spelman, Jimmy Clough and Terry Johnson have in common?

447.   Name all the Southend players born in Australia.

448.   Simon Francis, Ian Benjamin and Martin Carruthers share the same birthplace. Where?

449.   Which Southend trialist, who played 16 minutes of one game, was born in Port Gentiel, Gabon?

450.   Peter Beadle, Jamal Campbell-Ryce, Chris Powell and Jay Smith were all born in the same London borough. Which one?

ADAM BARRETT

451. In what position does Adam play for Southend?

452. What squad number did Adam wear for Southend during 2006/07?

453. In which year did Adam sign for Southend United?

454. From which team did he sign to join Southend?

455. Which manager signed Adam and gave him his Southend debut?

456. Against which club did Adam make his Southend debut in a 2-0 away defeat?

457. Against which former club did Adam score his first League goal for Southend, in a 2-1 away defeat?

458. How many League goals did Adam score for Southend in his first season at Roots Hall - 8, 10 or 12?

459. In January 2006 Adam scored in a 4-1 home win against Brentford. Which three players scored the other goals?

460. In August 2006, against which northeast-based side did Adam score a brace in a 3-1 home win?

DIVISION 4 RUNNERS-UP 1972

461. Who was manager of Southend during this season?

462. Which player finished as top goalscorer (in all competitions)?

463. Which team finished as champions of Division Four?

464. How many of their 46 League games did Southend win?

465. Can you name the other two teams that got promoted, finishing third and fourth?

466. Against which team did Southend get their first win of season, 3-0 at home?

467. Which player scored a hat-trick in March 1972 at home to Chester City?

468. True or false: Southend won all of their five League games during January 1972?

469. Against which club did Southend record their biggest home League crowd?

470. Who was Southend chairman during this season?

DAVE WEBB

471. In what year was David first appointed manager at Roots Hall?

472. Which team did David manage between 1980 and 1982?

473. How many spells as Southend manager has David had?

474. During David's playing days, in what position did he play?

475. What is David's nickname?

476. For which London team did David play between 1968 and 1974?

477. Which Southend chairman persuaded David to join the club from Yeovil Town in 2000?

478. Which team did David leave as manager to join Southend as boss for the very first time?

479. In what year was David born in London - 1936, 1946 or 1956?

480. To which Divison did David guide Southend in 1990?

PETER TAYLOR

481. Where was Peter born in 1953?

482. During Peter's playing days, in what position did he play?

483. What is Peter's nickname at Southend?

484. How many League games did Peter play for Southend in his career - 75, 175 or 375?

485. How many League goals did Peter score for Southend during his playing days - 2, 12 or 22?

486. For which London club did Peter play between 1976 and 1980?

487. In what year was Peter appointed manager?

488. When Peter left Southend as manager in 1995, who took over as boss?

489. In April 1971 Peter scored in a 3-0 home win in Division Four, against which side?

490. Which London club did Peter take charge of in 2006?

SPENCER PRIOR

491. In what year did Spencer sign for Southend (second spell)?

492. What is Spencer's middle name - Jamie, Justin or Jay?

493. What nationality is Spencer?

494. What is Spencer's nickname?

495. What was Spencer's squad number during 2006/07?

496. Spencer scored two League goals during 2004/05. Can you name the two sides he scored against?

497. Which manager gave Spencer his Southend debut at the club (first spell)?

498. In what position did Spencer play for Southend?

499. Which East Anglian team signed Spencer from Southend in June 1993?

500. When Spencer signed for Southend (second spell), from which club did he sign?

1980/81 CHAMPIONSHIP WINNING SEASON

501. Only one hat-trick was scored in the season. In a home game against which club did Derek Spence take home the match ball?

502. Which club did Southend defeat home and away by five goals to one?

503. Which club obliged Southend with an own goal in both the home and away fixtures?

504. Against which side did Southend play in front of the season's highest crowd of 11,965 at Roots Hall?

505. Southend went out in the opening round of the FA Cup to a side in the same division as them. Which club?

506. How many players did Dave Smith utilise during all 49 first team matches that season?

507. Derek Spence was top scorer with how many League and Cup goals?

508. Following on from the previous question, who followed him in the scoring stakes with 17?

509. For how many consecutive home matches did Mervyn Cawston keep a clean sheet?

510. How many League goals did Southend concede during the 23 home matches?

2005/06 CHAMPIONSHIP WINNING SEASON

511. For a match against which club did Roots Hall's largest gate of the season, 11,387, gather?

512. Shaun Goater made his final appearance in the English game against which club prior to retiring?

513. Four Southend players were credited with own goals during the season. Name them.

514. Southend picked up just two red cards in the campaign. Who got them?

515. Who made his Southend debut in the opening game of the season against Port Vale?

516. What did Daryl Flahavan accuse Dean Windass of doing at the match at Bradford City in August?

517. Who scored the goal that confirmed Southend would be crowned as champions?

518. Who opened the scoring in the 4-1 home win over Brentford?

519. Who scored the four second-half goals in the 4-1 demolition of Yeovil Town?

520. Freddy Eastwood was top scorer with 25 League and Cup goals. Who was the only other man to reach double figures?

TESTIMONIAL MATCHES

MATCH THE CORRECT SOUTHEND PLAYER WITH HIS TESTIMONIAL OPPONENTS

521.	West Ham United	Paul Clark
522.	Fulham	Tony Bentley
523.	Aston Villa	Arthur Rowley
524.	Charlton Athletic	Peter Watson
525.	England XI	Jimmy Lawler
526.	Stoke City	Dave Robinson
527.	Leicester City	Ronnie Pountney
528.	Middlesbrough	Steve Tilson
529.	Arsenal	Alan Moody
530.	Portsmouth	Frank Walton

SHIRT SPONSORS

MATCH THE SPONSOR TO THE CORRECT SEASON

531.	Progressive Printing	1987/88
532.	Access	1995/96
533.	Firholm	1985/86
534.	Betterview	1994/95
535.	Elonex	2005/06
536.	Crevette Clothing	1990/91
537.	Rebus	1998/99
538.	United Artists	1993/94
539.	Hi-Tec	1980/81
540.	Laing	2001/02

·

UNUSUAL LEAGUE RESULTS

541.   An 8-1 victory has only happened once, against whom?

542.   A 6-2 victory has only happened once, against whom?

543.   An 8-2 victory has only happened once, against whom?

544.   A 9-2 victory has only happened once, against whom?

545.   A 5-4 victory has only happened once, against whom?

546.   A 12-0 victory has only happened once, against whom?

547.   A 0-7 defeat has only happened once, against whom?

548.   A 0-8 defeat has only happened once, against whom?

549.   A 1-9 defeat has only happened once, against whom?

550.   A 1-11 defeat has only happened once, against whom?

SQUAD NUMBERS 2006/07

MATCH THE PLAYER WITH THE SQUAD NUMBER
HE WORE DURING THE SEASON

551.	Lee Bradbury	22
552.	Mark Gower	5
553.	Simon Francis	7
554.	Freddy Eastwood	12
555.	Kevin Maher	6
556.	Jay Smith	15
557.	Luke Guttridge	2
558.	Adam Barrett	8
559.	Michael Ricketts	10
560.	Spencer Prior	14

WHAT WAS THE SCORE? - 2

MATCH UP THE FIXTURE WITH THE FINAL SCORE

561.	*9 September 1989* *Aldershot (A), Division Four*	*4-2*
562.	*22 August 2000* *Birmingham City (H), League Cup*	*4-0*
563.	*1 January 1992* *Newcastle United (H), Division Two*	*0-5*
564.	*2 April 2004* *Scunthorpe United (H), Division Three*	*5-0*
565.	*5 March 1996* *Charlton Athletic (A), Division One*	*4-3*
566.	*16 October 1993* *Oxford United (H), Division One*	*0-5*
567.	*9 February 2007* *Queens Park Rangers (H), Championship*	*4-2*
568.	*13 October 2001* *Swansea City (H), Division Three*	*6-1*
569.	*1 October 1997* *Derby County (A), League Cup*	*5-0*
570.	*1 May 1994* *Derby County (H), Division One*	*3-0*

DARRYL FLAHAVAN

571. In what year did Darryl sign for Southend?

572. From which team did Darryl sign to join Southend?

573. Darryl made his Southend debut against which club in a 3-1 away League defeat?

574. What nationality is Darryl?

575. Where was Darryl born in 1978?

576. Which two awards did Darryl win at the end of the 2005/06 season?

577. What is Darryl's nickname?

578. What squad number did Darryl wear during 2006/07?

579. Which manager signed Darryl and handed him his Southend debut?

580. In what position does Darryl play?

ROB NEWMAN

581.   In what position did Rob play during his playing days?

582.   In what year did Rob sign for Southend?

583.   At which club did Rob start his career as an apprentice, leaving them in 1991?

584.   Following on from the previous question, which club did he join and played there for 7 years?

585.   Against which team did Rob make his Southend debut, in a 2-1 away win?

586.   Rob scored his first goal for Southend in a 1-0 win in the League Cup, only his second game for the club. Which team did Southend beat?

587.   How many League goals did Rob score for Southend in his first season at Roots Hall?

588.   In what year was Rob appointed Southend United manager?

589.   What is Rob's middle name - Kevin, Ronny or Nigel?

590.   Which club appointed Rob as manager in 2005?

STEVE TILSON

591. In what year did Steve take over as Southend manager (as caretaker)?

592. From which club did Southend buy Steve in February 1989 - Witham Town, Wivenhoe or Clacton Town?

593. During his playing career in what position did Steve play?

594. In which year was Steve born - 1964, 1966 or 1968?

595. Which manager signed Steve for Southend in 1989?

596. Following on from Q591, which manager did Steve take over from, who was in temporary charge - David Webb, Peter Taylor or Steve Wignall?

597. During the 2004/05 season, to which position in the League did Steve guide Southend?

598. In October 1996 Steve scored in a 1-0 home win against which side - Oldham, Grimsby Town or Manchester City?

599. Following on from Q591, which Southend chairman offered Steve the caretaker manager's and then the permanent job a year later?

600. What is Steve's nickname - Tilly, Tully or ST?

2004/05 PLAY-OFF FINAL

601. In which minutes did Freddy Eastwood and Duncan Jupp score for Southend?

602. What was the attendance at the Millennium Stadium?

603. Who was the only Southend player to be cautioned in the final?

604. Who were the two unused substitutes on the day?

605. Who refereed the match?

606. Lincoln had a goal ruled out for offside after 29 minutes. Who was the unfortunate Lincoln player?

607. Who replaced Wayne Gray eight minutes before the end of normal time?

608. What shirt number did Mark Bentley wear in the final?

609. What kit did Southend wear?

610. Which Southend player's header was deflected into Freddy Eastwood's path for the opening goal?

ANGLO-ITALIAN CUP

611.   Who were Southend's first opponents in the competition in September 1992?

612.   What was the margin of the penalty defeat to Notts County in the 1994/95 semi-final?

613.   Who were the first Italian opponents to play at Roots Hall in November 1994?

614.   Who scored Southend's first goal in the competition?

615.   Who has scored more Anglo-Italian Cup goals for Southend than any other player?

616.   Southend's only victory on Italian soil came at Cosenza. Who scored the goals in the 2-1 triumph?

617.   In October 1995, Southend played Reggiana in Italy. What was the name of the stadium the match was played in?

618.   Who scored in the 2-1 defeat at Salernitana in November 1995?

619.   Which opponents in this competition attracted the biggest Roots Hall attendance?

620.   What happened to Ricky Otto at the end of the match in Cosenza?

WHERE DID THEY GO?

MATCH THE FOLLOWING PLAYERS WITH THE CLUB
THEY JOINED AFTER LEAVING SOUTHEND

621.	Avery Osmond	Wolverhampton Wanderers
622.	Chris Powell	Glenavon
623.	Stuart Brace	Betteshanger Colliery Welfare
624.	Paul Byrne	Fisher Athletic
625.	Lee Chapman	Stevenage Borough
626.	Jason Harris	Walsall
627.	Adrian Clarke	Derby County
628.	Andy Rammell	Nuneaton Borough
629.	Shane Westley	Falmouth Town
630.	Mark Warren	Ipswich Town

CUP RUNS

631. In 1979/80 Southend reached the third round of the League Cup. Who did they put out in round one?

632. In the 1982/83 FA Cup Southend went out in the third round, but which non-League side did they defeat on the way?

633. Who put Southend out of the Littlewoods Cup at the third round stage in 1987/88?

634. In the 1990/91 Leyland Daf Cup run, how many goals were scored in the five matches played?

635. Who put Southend out of their only season in the Zenith Data Systems Cup in 1991?

636. Southend went out to Kingstonian in the third round of the 2000/01 FA Cup, but which League side did they defeat in the opening round?

637. Southend were LDV Trophy finalists in 2003/04, but who did they defeat in the first round?

638. Southend were LDV Trophy finalists in 2004/05, but who did they defeat in the first round?

639. Southend reached the fifth round of the FA Cup in 1975/76. Who were their only non-League opponents in that run?

640. Southend played Liverpool famously in the 1978/79 FA Cup competition, but who did they eliminate in the opening round that season?

POSITIONS IN THE LEAGUE

641. Name the two Football League seasons in which the club were forced to apply for re-election to the Football League?

642. In which three campaigns did the club finished rooted to the foot of the table for the division they were in?

643. Southend were promoted from Division 4 in 1977/78. In which position in the table did they finish?

644. In which season did Southend achieve their highest ever final placing in the Football League?

645. What was Southend's highest placing in the old Third Division South?

646. When Southend were promoted from the Third Division in 1989/90, what was their final League placing?

647. In what position did Southend finish in the 2003/04 Division Three campaign?

648. In their first season in the Fourth Division in 1966/67, where did Southend finish in the League campaign?

649. Name the two seasons in which Southend topped the table at the end of a League season?

650. Name the only season in which Southend qualified for the end-of-season play-off matches?

TOP LEAGUE GOALSCORERS IN A SEASON

651.	1990/91	Billy Best (31)
652.	2005/06	Jack Moffitt (21)
653.	1982/83	Leon Constantine (25)
654.	1993/94	David Crown (29)
655.	1968/69	Brett Angell (26)
656.	2003/04	Steve Phillips (17)
657.	1963/64	Albert Wakefield (28)
658.	1988/89	Ricky Otto (15)
659.	1949/50	Micky Beesley (13)
660.	1932/33	Freddy Eastwood (25)

SANDY ANDERSON

661. In what position did Sandy play for Southend in his playing days?

662. In what year was Sandy born - 1910, 1920 or 1930?

663. How many League goals did Sandy score for Southend in his career - 2, 8 or 14?

664. When Sandy left Roots Hall, which club did he join?

665. How many League appearances did Sandy make for Southend in his career - 252, 352 or 452?

666. In April 1951 Sandy scored in a 3-2 home win in Division Three South, against which team?

667. Which Southend manager gave Sandy his debut?

668. In August 1952 Sandy scored in a 3-1 away win in Division Three South, against which team?

669. Which record does Sandy currently hold for Southend?

670. Who was the manager when Sandy played his last game for Southend?

ALAN LITTLE

671.   In what year was Alan born - 1950, 1955 or 1960?

672.   In what position did Alan play during his playing days?

673.   In what year did Alan sign for Southend?

674.   Which manager signed Alan for Southend?

675.   For how much did Southend buy Alan from Aston Villa - £5,000, £10,000 or £20,000?

676.   Which team bought Alan from Southend in 1977?

677.   In what year was Alan appointed Southend boss?

678.   How many League goals did Alan score in his Southend career?

679.   Which team did Alan manage between 1993 and 1999?

680.   What is the name of Alan's brother who also played at Aston Villa at the same time as Alan?

DIVISION 4 RUNNERS-UP 1978

681.   Who was manager of Southend during this season?

682.   Who was player of the season?

683.   Southend played Reading on the opening day of the League season, Southend winning the game 1-0, but who scored?

684.   Which player scored four goals in a 4-0 home win in September 1977 against Torquay United?

685.   Behind which team did Southend finish?

686.   Can you name the other two teams that gained promotion, finishing third and fourth?

687.   How many of the 46 League games did Southend win - 23, 25 or 27?

688.   Southend won all 4 games during February 1978, can you name two of the 4 sides they beat?

689.   Can you name the team that Southend beat 2-1 on the last day of the season?

690.   Following on from the previous question, can you name the two goalscorers?

LDV VANS TROPHY
RUNNERS-UP 2005

691. Who managed Southend during this Cup run?

692. Which player scored the goal in the first round in September 2004 in the 1-1 draw at Layer Road against Colchester United?

693. In November 2004, which team did Southend beat 4-1 at home in the second round?

694. Following on from the previous question, which player scored a brace in the game?

695. Which team did Southend play in the third round in a 2-0 home win?

696. Which team did Southend play in the fourth round, a 2-0 home win, with Lawrie Dudfield and Nicky Nicolau scoring the goals?

697. Which two players scored the goals in the semi-final home 2-2 draw against Bristol Rovers?

698. Following on from the previous question, what was the aggreate score after playing both matches in the semi-final?

699. Who were the opponents in the final, losing 2-0?

700. In which stadium was the final held?

SOUTHEND IN THE ASSOCIATE MEMBERS' CLUB

701.   Name Southend's three opponents in the 1981/82 Football League Group Cup?

702.   Name Southend's three opponents in the 1982/83 Football League Trophy?

703.   Southend's first Associate Members' Cup tie came on 20/2/1983 against Reading. What was the final score and what was significant about the match programme?

704.   In the 1983/84 match against Bristol Rovers at Roots Hall, what did Southend physio Buster Footman do which hit the headlines?

705.   Who scored the only Southend goal of the 1984/85 Freight Rover Trophy campaign against Millwall?

706.   In the 1986/87 tournament, which two sides did Southend defeat in the opening group stage?

707.   What was the competition known as in the 1988/89 season when Southend went out to Northampton Town after extra time?

708.   Who scored the "golden goal" extra time winner against Swindon Town in February 2001?

709.   What was significant about the seven goals Southend scored in the Leyland Daf Cup tie against Torquay in February 1991?

710.   Name the three Southend players who have scored a hat-trick in this competition?

LOAN PLAYERS

711. Which left back came on loan from Sheffield Wednesday in March 1985?

712. Name the two Football League clubs to which James Lawson was loaned during the 2006/07 campaign.

713. Which diminutive winger came to the club on loan from Tottenham Hotspur in March 1996?

714. Name the only player to have had three different loan spells at the club?

715. Who played one game for Southend while on loan from West Ham United in January 1995?

716. Name the West Ham centre back that played one minute as a substitute whilst on loan during the 2005/06 season?

717. Which defensive midfielder arrived on loan from Preston North End in February 2002?

718. Name the midfielder signed on loan from Notts County in August 1993?

719. In December 2002, Danny Marney arrived on loan from which club?

720. Which midfielder arrived on loan from Sheffield Wednesday in February 1997?

UNUSUAL SOURCES

EACH PLAYER BELOW WAS THE ONLY ONE TO BE SIGNED FROM THEIR CLUB BY SOUTHEND - MATCH THEM UP

721.	Greig Shepherd	Backworth Percy
722.	Buck Fryar	Benburb Star
723.	Andy Thomson	Brechin City
724.	Sandy Anderson	CD Numancia
725.	Graham Franklin	Eastern Athletic
726.	Dave Cunningham	Newburgh Juniors
727.	Jimmy Clark	Queen of the South
728.	Nathan Jones	Saffron Walden Town
729.	Joe Hall	Shoebury Town
730.	Scott Forbes	Lowestoft Town

KEVIN MAHER

731. In which town was Kevin born?

732. In what year did Kevin sign for Southend?

733. True or false: Kevin has been capped by Ireland at under-21 level?

734. Which Southend manager brought Kevin to the club?

735. Against whom did Kevin make his Southend debut?

736. In which two seasons did Kevin bag his personal best tally of five goals in a campaign?

737. Kevin was voted Player of the Year in which two seasons?

738. Which manager made Kevin club captain at Roots Hall?

739. How many yellow cards did Kevin receive during 2002/03 - 12, 13 or 14?

740. In which two seasons was Kevin elected to the PFA Divisional team of the year?

TOTAL APPEARANCES FOR SOUTHEND UNITED

MATCH THE PLAYER WITH THE TOTAL NUMBER OF FIRST TEAM APPEARANCES MADE FOR THE CLUB

741.	Harry Threadgold	304
742.	Tony Hadley	401
743.	Tony Bentley	357
744.	Chris Powell	343
745.	Paul Clark	342
746.	Alan Moody	483
747.	Billy Moore	290
748.	Sandy Anderson	358
749.	Paul Sansome	419
750.	Ronnie Pountney	507

ANDY SMILLIE

751. In what year was Andy born - 1931, 1941 or 1951?

752. In what year did Andy make his debut for Southend?

753. Which manager handed Andy his Southend debut?

754. How many League goals did Andy score during his Southend career?

755. In December 1964 Andy scored a brace in a 3-1 away win, against which team?

756. In May 1966 Andy scored the only goal in a 1-0 League win against which team?

757. From which team did Southend sign Andy?

758. In March 1968, which team did Southend beat 7-0 in a Division Four win, with Andy scoring one of the goals?

759. How many games did Andy play for Southend (in all competitions) - 80, 180 or 280?

760. In November 1964 Andy scored the only goal in a 1-0 away win, against which club?

JOHN McKINVEN

761. In what position did John play for Southend in his playing days?

762. In which year did John join Southend?

763. From which club did John sign to join Southend?

764. What nationality is John?

765. How many League goals did John score for Southend?

766. John scored his first goal for Southend in October 1960 in a 1-1 draw away from home, against which club?

767. In December 1962, against which team did John score a brace in a 5-1 home win?

768. John scored in a 2-1 home win against Halifax Town, but who scored the other goal?

769. In November 1964 John scored a brace in the 6-3 home win against Colchester United, but which player scored the other four goals?

770. Which injury sadly ended John's career in a tackle made by Graham Taylor?

BILL GARNER

771.   In what year was Bill born in Leicester?

772.   In what position did Bill play during his playing days?

773.   What nationality is Bill?

774.   At which club did Bill start his career before joining Southend?

775.   True or false: Bill was Southend's first £100,000 player?

776.   In what year did Bill sign for Southend?

777.   Which Southend manager signed Bill for the club?

778.   How many League goals did Bill score for the club - 21, 31 or 41?

779.   How many League appearances did Bill make for Southend - 82, 102 or 122?

780.   For which London club did Bill sign when he left Roots Hall in 1972?

RON POUNTNEY

781. In what year was Ron born - 1950, 1955 or 1960?

782. How many League goals did Ron score for Southend in his career - 16, 26 or 36?

783. When Ron left Roots Hall in 1985, which Essex-based side did he join?

784. Which manager brought Ron to Southend?

785. In what position did Ron play during his Southend playing days?

786. True or false: Ron won Southend Player of the Year on three ocassions?

787. Ron played his testimonial match in 2000, against which London-based Premier League side?

788. In October 1978 Ron scored in a 4-0 Division Three win at Roots Hall, against which team?

789. Can you name the four managers that Ron played under at the club?

790. How much did Ron cost Southend?

RICHARD CADETTE

791. True or false: Richard won Southend United Player of the Year in his first season at the club?

792. In what position did Richard play for Southend?

793. How many League goals did Richard score for Southend?

794. In which year did Richard join Southend?

795. From which London club did Richard sign to join Southend?

796. Against which team did Richard score four goals in a 5-1 home win in the League during 1985?

797. Which Southend manager signed Richard for the club?

798. In May 1986 Richard scored a hat-trick in a 5-0 home League win, against which team?

799. In which competition did Richard score a hat-trick in the 4-4 home draw in December 1986?

800. For which team did Richard sign when he left Roots Hall?

ANSWERS

GOALSCORERS

1. *Jimmy Shankly (34 in 1928/29)*
2. *Roy Hollis (1954/55, 1955/56 and 1956/57)*
3. *Freddy Eastwood (7.7 seconds v. Swansea, 16/10/2004)*
4. *Billy Best (9)*
5. *He was also top scorer in the same season for his previous club Cambridge United*
6. *It was fullback Jimmy Evans with 10 penalties*
7. *Roy Hollis (135)*
8. *Emlyn "Mickey" Jones*
9. *Albert Fairclough (v. Bristol City, 28/08/1920)*
10. *Billy Hick (15/10/1927 to 19/11/1927)*

WHO AM I?

11. *Stuart Parker*
12. *Roy McDonough*
13. *Shaun Goater*
14. *Paul Sansome*
15. *Jimmy Shankly*
16. *Tony Bentley*
17. *Stan Collymore*
18. *Chris Powell*
19. *Gary Moore*
20. *Ronnie Pountney*

ROOTS HALL

21. *Sid Broomfield*
22. *13,500*
23. *Boulton and Paul of Norwich*
24. *1994*
25. *1955*
26. *1959*
27. *£73,997*
28. *v. Liverpool in 1979 (31,033)*
29. *Old Trafford*
30. *True*

EARLY DAYS

31. *Oliver Trigg*
32. *The Blue Boar Public House*
33. *Bob Jack*

34. William "Jerry" Thomson
35. George Molyneux
36. Blue shirts with black collars and cuffs, and white shorts
37. 222
38. He was knowingly played under a pseudonym - he was actually Billy Askew, a player serving a lengthy ban from the sport
39. Bradford Park Avenue
40. They adopted a kit of brown and yellow hoops

CUP TIES
41. Bolton Wanderers (League Cup, second round, 1979)
42. Doncaster Rovers (November 1998)
43. Billy Best and Gary Moore scored hat-tricks in both rounds
44. Everton at Goodison Park (January 1955)
45. 1975/76
46. Blackpool (LDV Vans Trophy final, March 2004)
47. East Ham (September 1907)
48. Barnet
49. It was the first Cup tie settled on the "golden goal" rule when Leo Roget scored the winning goal
50. Richard Cadette

MARK GOWER
51. 1978
52. Barnet
53. Motherwell
54. Tottenham Hotspur
55. 7
56. Ipswich Town
57. Peter Clarke
58. 6
59. Norwich City
60. Queens Park Rangers

SOUTHEND MANAGERS
61.	Bobby Moore	1984-1986
62.	Ronnie Whelan	1995-1997
63.	Alan Little	1999-2000
64.	Stewart Robson	2003
65.	Ted Fenton	1961-1965
66.	Dave Smith	1976-1983

67.	Barry Fry	1993
68.	Peter Taylor	1993-1995
69.	Steve Wignall	2003
70.	Ted Birnie	1921-1934

NATIONALITIES

71.	Efe Sodje	Nigerian
72.	Spencer Prior	English
73.	Jamal Campbell-Ryce	Jamaican
74.	Franck Moussa	Belgian
75.	Steven Hammell	Scottish
76.	Lee Bradbury	English
77.	Kevin Maher	Republic of Ireland
78.	Alan McCormack	Republic of Ireland
79.	Richie Foran	Republic of Ireland
80.	Stan Collymore	English

SOUTHEND GOALKEEPERS

81.	Darryl Flahavan
82.	Martyn Margetson and Melvyn Capleton
83.	Steve Collis
84.	Darryl Flahavan and Bart Griemink
85.	Andy Woodman
86.	Danny Gay
87.	9
88.	Mervyn Cawston
89.	Notts County
90.	Joe Welch

2006/07

91.	Stoke City
92.	Freddy Eastwood
93.	Adam Barrett
94.	Steve Tilson
95.	Manchester United
96.	Freddy Eastwood and Alan McCormack
97.	West Bromwich Albion
98.	Mark Gower
99.	Ron Martin
100.	Tottenham Hotspur

APPEARANCES

101.   Alan Moody (507)
102.   Alex "Sandy" Anderson (452)
103.   Alan Moody (33)
104.   Dave Martin (25)
105.   Steve Tilson (47)
106.   Arthur Williamson
107.   Paul Sansome
108.   Peter Daley (5)
109.   Mervyn Cawston, Terry Gray and Derek Spence
110.   Jim Stannard, Paul Clark and Richard Cadette

AGES

111.   Mick Gooding
112.   Neville Southall
113.   Phil O'Connor
114.   Franck Moussa
115.   Shaun Goater
116.   Frank Lampard
117.   Mick Gooding
118.   Bobby Kellard
119.   Richard Jobson (January), Rob Newman (August)
120.   Trevor Whymark

ATTENDANCES

121.   21,020, v. Leyton Orient, 03/05/1955
122.   The Anglo Italian Cup tie at Cosenza
123.   1958/59
124.   1984/85
125.   683, v. Northampton Town, Freight Rover Trophy, 13/03/1986
126.   1,006, v. Halifax Town, 05/03/1986
127.   Yeovil Town, 30/04/2005 (11,735)
128.   935, v. Wrexham, 30/04/1987
129.   35,689, v. Notts County 26/03/1948
130.   Wrexham, 10/04/2005 (36,216), Blackpool, 21/03/2004, attracted 34,031

INTERNATIONALS

131.   Lot Jones
132.   Efe Sodje
133.   St Kitts and Nevis

134.   George McKenzie (9)
135.   Ronnie Whelan
136.   Sammy McCrory and Tes Bramble
137.   Jimmy McAlinden, Sammy McCrory and Derek Spence
138.   Harold Halse, Peter Taylor, Stan Collymore and Chris Powell
139.   Charlie Turner and George McKenzie
140.   Dominic Foley

GROUNDS
141.   Wealdstone (1979)
142.   Woking (1997)
143.   Workington (1964-1977)
144.   Watford (1908-1922)
145.   AP Leamington (1974 and 1977)
146.   Barrow (1967, 1971 and 1972)
147.   Walthamstow Avenue (1937)
148.   Brush Sports (1946)
149.   Queens Park Rangers (1908-1919)
150.   Corinthians (1937) and Queens Park Rangers (1963)

MATCH THE YEAR
151.	League One champions	2006
152.	League Two play-off winners	2005
153.	Division Four runners-up	1972
154.	LDV Vans Trophy runners-up	2004
155.	Highest attendance of 31,033 against Liverpool in the FA Cup	1979
156.	Division Three runners-up	1991
157.	Division Four runners-up	1978
158.	LDV Vans Trophy runners-up	2005
159.	Stan Collymore signs for Southend	1992
160.	Division Four champions	1981

WHAT WAS THE SCORE? - 1
161.	3 November 1979 Carlisle United (A), Division Three	0-4
162.	29 April 1952 Ipswich Town (H), Division Three South	5-0
163.	21 November 1970 Weymouth (H), FA Cup	7-0

164.	12 September 1962	
	Shrewsbury Town (A), Division Three	0-6
165.	2 September 1974	
	Halifax Town (H), Division Three	4-0
166.	24 November 1951	
	Bournemouth & BA (H), FA Cup	6-1
167.	22 February 1975	
	Wrexham (A), Division Three	1-7
168.	13 October 1951	
	Aldershot (H), Division Three South	7-1
169.	29 March 1968	
	Workington (H), Division Four	7-0
170.	17 February 1976	
	Brighton & Hove Albion (H), Division Three	4-0

DIVISION 3 RUNNERS-UP 1991

171. Peter Butler
172. David Webb
173. Brett Angell
174. 26
175. Huddersfield Town
176. Cambridge United
177. Brentford
178. Brett Angell
179. Cambridge United
180. 14

CHRIS POWELL

181. Crystal Palace
182. Defender
183. Exeter City
184. David Webb
185. 5
186. Ronnie Whelan
187. Watford
188. Charlton Athletic
189. Luton Town
190. Derby County

TONY BENTLEY

191. Defender (fullback)

192. *Stoke City*
193. *419: 417 (2)*
194. *1965/66*
195. *17*
196. *1939*
197. *Ted Fenton*
198. *Notts County*
199. *Walsall*
200. *John Baber*

MANAGERS

201. *Tom Mather*
202. *Mick Gooding*
203. *Rob Newman*
204. *Arthur Rowley*
205. *Stewart Robson*
206. *Major Alf Hay*
207. *George Molyneux, David Jack, Frank Broome, Bobby Moore, Peter Taylor and Alvin Martin*
208. *Dave Smith*
209. *Frank Broome*
210. *Colin Murphy*

EXOTIC FRIENDLIES

211. *France*
212. *Belgium*
213. *Malta*
214. *Italy (Sicily)*
215. *Germany*
216. *Czechoslovakia*
217. *Holland*
218. *Germany*
219. *Soviet Union*
220. *Holland*

TRANSFERS OUT

221. *Ricky Otto*
222. *Brett Angell*
223. *Dean Austin*
224. *Jason Lee*
225. *Mark McNally*

226. Colin Morris
227. Peter Taylor
228. Barry Conlon
229. Leo Roget
230. Ian Hamilton

TRANSFERS IN

231. Gary Poole
232. Andy Rammell
233. Andy Thomson
234. Keith Jones
235. Mike Lapper
236. Ricky Otto
237. Tommy Mooney
238. Keith Mercer
239. Mark Rawle
240. David Roche

HAT-TRICKS

241. Brett Angell (4) and Steve Tilson (3)
242. Leon Cort
243. Tommy Mooney (v. Oxford, Oct. 1993) and Julian Hails (v. Leicester, Sept. 1995)
244. Richard Cadette
245. Roy Hollis and Jimmy Shankly
246. 3
247. Andy Ansah
248. 3
249. Derrick Parker
250. Newport County and Norwich City

SIMON ROYCE

251. Heybridge Swifts
252. Goalkeeper
253. Charlton Athletic
254. 1971
255. English
256. David Webb
257. Alvin Martin
258. Leicester City
259. £10,000

260. Queens Park Rangers

DAVID CROWN
261. Centre forward
262. Cambridge United
263. 113
264. Paul Clark
265. 61
266. York City
267. True
268. Reading
269. Gillingham
270. Aldershot

FREDDY EASTWOOD
271. 1983
272. Grays Athletic
273. 6
274. 24
275. Huddersfield Town
276. Bristol City and Chesterfield
277. Swansea City
278. Kevin Maher and Che Wilson
279. 2005/06
280. Steve Tilson

BILLY BEST
281. Northampton Town
282. 2
283. Halifax Town
284. Ernie Shepherd
285. 7
286. True
287. August (v. Scunthorpe United)
288. Aldershot
289. 22
290. True

ALAN MOODY
291. The most appearances for the club (507)
292. 1951

293. 446: 444 (2)
294. 41
295. Defender
296. Maldon Town
297. Arthur Rowley
298. 4: Arthur Rowley, Dave Smith, Peter Morris and Bobby Moore
299. He won the Southend Player of the Year award
300. West Ham United

GOALSCORING DEBUTS

301. Mark Gower
302. Shaun Goater
303. Lawrie Dudfield
304. Martin Robinson
305. Stan Collymore
306. Lee Chapman
307. Brighton and Hove Albion
308. Steve Phillips, as he failed to score on his debut
309. Jason Lee and Tommy Mooney
310. Martin Ling

STAN COLLYMORE

311. Cannock
312. Stafford Rangers
313. Huddersfield Town
314. Liverpool and Bradford City
315. Japan
316. Frank Clark
317. Roy Evans
318. Tackling my Demons
319. La Manga
320. 3 (all as substitute)

BARRY FRY

321. Bookmaker
322. Bolton Wanderers
323. Leyton Orient
324. Bedford Town
325. George Best
326. Stan Flashman
327. Eddie Stein and Dave Howell

328. 3-1 to Southend
329. Andy Edwards, Dave Howell, Jonathan Hunt, Jae Martin, Ricky Otto and Gary Poole
330. Peter Boizot

SHAUN GOATER

331. Hamilton
332. Leonard
333. North Village
334. Manchester United
335. Rotherham United
336. Bristol City
337. Joe Royle
338. Manchester United
339. Coventry City
340. Colchester United and Tranmere Rovers

RED CARDS

341. Julian Hails, Mick Gooding and Kevin Maher
342. David McSweeney, Jay Smith and Mark Gower
343. Leon Cort and Mark Rawle
344. 5
345. Roy McDonough
346. 2003/04
347. Mick Bodley
348. 3
349. Mark Beard and Rob Newman
350. Mark Rawle

RICKY OTTO

351. 1993
352. 17
353. Barry Fry
354. Birmingham City
355. £800,000
356. 1967
357. False: he is English
358. Leyton Orient
359. Winger
360. Peter Taylor

ROY McDONOUGH

361.   Centre forward (Centre back on occasions)
362.   2
363.   1983
364.   38
365.   1958
366.   Colchester United
367.   Preston North End
368.   Brian Ferguson and Steve Phillips
369.   English
370.   7

POSITIONS IN THE LEAGUE

371.   1991/92   12th in Division Two
372.   2005/06   1st in League One
373.   1996/97   24th in Division One
374.   1987/88   17th in Division Three
375.   2002/03   17th in Division Three
376.   1979/80   22nd in Division Three
377.   1963/64   14th in Division Three
378.   1993/94   15th in Division One
379.   2000/01   11th in Division Three
380.   1926/27   19th in Division Three South

POT LUCK

381.   Alvan Williams
382.   Derby County
383.   1906
384.   £3.57 million
385.   The Shrimpers, The Seasiders and The Blues
386.   1955
387.   Rotherham United
388.   True
389.   Victor
390.   True

LDV VANS TROPHY RUNNERS-UP 2004

391.   Steve Tilson
392.   Bristol Rovers
393.   Leon Constantine and Mark Gower
394.   2-1 to Southend

395. Luton Town
396. Queens Park Rangers
397. Colchester United
398. 4-3 (3-2 and 1-1)
399. Darryl Flahavan, Duncan Jupp, Che Wilson, Lewis Hunt, Mark Warren, Leon Cort, Carl Pettefer, Kevin Maher, Drewe Broughton, Mark Gower and Leon Constantine
400. The Millennium Stadium

BITS AND PIECES

401. Arsenal
402. Both matches were delayed as the grandstand had caught fire
403. The floodlights failed
404. New Writtle Street, Chelmsford City FC
405. Bright's Disease
406. 1960 and 1966
407. Bobby Gilfillan
408. Southend Invicta
409. Rabbit poaching
410. Throwing mud at a penalty taker

OVERSEAS PLAYERS

411. Cape Town, South Africa — Eddie Firmani
412. Arnheim, Holland — Jeroen Boere
413. Redondo Beach, United States — Mike Lapper
414. Montreal, Canada — Errol Crossan
415. Brignoles, France — Regis Coulbault
416. Brussels, Belgium — Franck Moussa
417. Lillehammer, Norway — Pettar Belsvik
418. Dakar, Senegal — Sada N'Diaye
419. Eutin, Germany — Lars Unger
420. Lagos, Nigeria — Dominic Iorfa

PLAYER OF THE YEAR

421. Ronnie Pountney
422. Billy Best
423. Alan Moody
424. Derek Spence
425. Micky Stead
426. Dave Martin
427. David Crown

428.   Simon Royce
429.   Keith Dublin
430.   Kevin Maher

NON-LEAGUE FA CUP TIES

431.	Trowbridge Town 0, Southend United 2	1957
432.	Ilford 0, Southend United 2	1974
433.	London Paper Mills 0, Southend United 1	1933
434.	Brush Sports 1, Southend United 6	1946
435.	Southend United 7, Weymouth 0	1970
436.	Southend United 4, Automotive Products Leamington 0	1977
437.	Southend United 1, Wellington Town 0	1927
438.	Finchley 1, Southend United 3	1953
439.	Southend United 6, Oswestry Town 0	1959
440.	Walthamstow Avenue 0, Southend United 1	1937

BIRTHPLACES

441.   18
442.   All born in Bellshill
443.   Jimmy McAlinden, Sammy McCrory, Sammy McMillen and Derek Spence
444.   All born in Hackney
445.   Lee Bradbury
446.   All born in Newcastle upon Tyne
447.   George Horsfall, John Roberts, Chris Coyne and Andy Petterson (strangely three of them only played one match)
448.   Nottingham
449.   Roger N'Zamba
450.   Lambeth

ADAM BARRETT

451.   Defender
452   6
453.   2004
454.   Bristol Rovers
455.   Steve Tilson
456.   Rochdale
457.   Bristol Rovers
458.   10
459.   Efe Sodje, Mark Gower and Che Wilson

460. *Sunderland*

DIVISION 4 RUNNERS-UP 1972
461. *Arthur Rowley*
462. *Bill Garner (26 goals)*
463. *Grimsby Town*
464. *24*
465. *Brentford and Scunthorpe United*
466. *Darlington*
467. *Bill Garner*
468. *False: won 2, lost 3*
469. *Cambridge United*
470. *Bill Rubin*

DAVID WEBB
471. *1986*
472. *Bournemouth*
473. *4*
474. *Defender (right-back)*
475. *DJ*
476. *Chelsea*
477. *Ron Martin*
478. *Torquay United*
479. *1946*
480. *Division Three*

PETER TAYLOR
481. *Southend*
482. *Midfielder/Winger*
483. *Spud*
484. *75: 57 (18)*
485. *12*
486. *Tottenham Hotspur*
487. *1993*
488. *Steve Thompson*
489. *Oldham Athletic*
490. *Crystal Palace*

SPENCER PRIOR
491. *2004*
492. *Justin*

493. English
494. Spinner
495. 5
496. Swansea City and Cambridge United
497. David Webb
498. Defender
499. Norwich City
500. Cardiff City

1980/81 CHAMPIONSHIP SEASON

501. York City
502. Halifax Town
503. Tranmere Rovers
504. Lincoln City
505. Hereford United
506. 17
507. 21
508. Terry Gray
509. 10
510. 6

2005/06 CHAMPIONSHIP WINNING SEASON

511. Bristol City
512. Bristol City
513. Jamal Campbell-Ryce (at Notts Forest), Duncan Jupp
      (at Brentford), Lewis Hunt and Kevin Maher (both at Barnsley)
514. Freddy Eastwood (at Huddersfield) and Adam Barrett (at Yeovil)
515. Mitchell Cole
516. Biting him
517. Wayne Gray
518. Efe Sodje
519. Luke Guttridge, Wayne Gray and Freddy Eastwood (2)
520. Shaun Goater (11)

TESTIMONIAL MATCHES

521.	West Ham United	Alan Moody
522.	Fulham	Peter Watson
523.	Aston Villa	Dave Robinson
524.	Charlton Athletic	Ronnie Pountney
525.	England XI	Steve Tilson
526.	Stoke City	Tony Bentley

527.	Leicester City	Arthur Rowley
528.	Middlesbrough	Frank Walton
529.	Arsenal	Paul Clark
530.	Portsmouth	Jimmy Lawler

SHIRT SPONSORS

531.	Progressive Printing	1998/99
532.	Access	1980/81
533.	Firholm	1987/88
534.	Betterview	2005/06
535.	Elonex	1993/94
536.	Crevette Clothing	1994/95
537.	Rebus	2001/02
538.	United Artists	1995/96
539.	Hi-Tec	1990/91
540.	Laing	1985/86

UNUSUAL LEAGUE RESULTS

541.	Cardiff City (H), 20/02/1937
542.	Newport County (H), 31/01/1931
543.	Swindon Town (H), 24/02/1951
544.	Newport County (H), 05/09/1936
545.	Queens Park Rangers (A), 11/01/1964
546.	Royal Engineers (H), 15/09/1906
547.	Sunderland (A), 03/11/1987
548.	Northampton Town (A), 22/03/1924
549.	Brighton and Hove Albion (A), 27/11/1965
550.	Northampton Town (A), 30/12/1909

SQUAD NUMBERS 2006/07

551.	Lee Bradbury	12
552.	Mark Gower	7
553.	Simon Francis	2
554.	Freddy Eastwood	10
555.	Kevin Maher	8
556.	Jay Smith	22
557.	Luke Guttridge	14
558.	Adam Barrett	6
559.	Michael Ricketts	15
560.	Spencer Prior	5

WHAT WAS THE SCORE? - 2

561.	9 September 1989	
	Aldershot (A), Division Four	5-0
562.	22 August 2000	
	Birmingham City (H), League Cup	0-5
563.	1 January 1992	
	Newcastle United (H), Division Two	4-0
564.	2 April 2004	
	Scunthorpe United (H), Division Three	4-2
565.	5 March 1996	
	Charlton Athletic (A), Division One	3-0
566.	16 October 1993	
	Oxford United (H), Division One	6-1
567.	9 February 2007	
	Queens Park Rangers (H), Championship	5-0
568.	13 October 2001	
	Swansea City (H), Division Three	4-2
569.	1 October 1997	
	Derby County (A), League Cup	0-5
570.	1 May 1994	
	Derby County (H), Division One	4-3

DARRYL FLAHAVAN

571. 2000
572. Woking
573. Carlisle
574. English
575. Southampton
576. PFA Player of the Year and Southend United Player of the Year
577. Flavs
578. 1
579. David Webb
580. Goalkeeper

ROB NEWMAN

581. Defender
582. 1998
583. Bristol City
584. Norwich City
585. Scarborough
586. Gillingham

587. 7
588. 2001
589. Nigel
590. Cambridge United

STEVE TILSON

591. 2003
592. Witham Town
593. Midfielder
594. 1966
595. David Webb
596. David Webb
597. 4th
598. Grimsby Town
599. Ron Martin
600. Tilly

2004/05 PLAY-OFF FINAL

601. 106 and 110
602. 19,653
603. Mark Bentley
604. Bart Griemink and Luke Guttridge
605. Mark Atkinson
606. Simon Yeo
607. Lawrie Dudfield
608. 9
609. All dark blue
610. Spencer Prior

ANGLO-ITALIAN CUP

611. Bristol Rovers
612. 3-4
613. Pescara
614. Derek Payne (v. Luton Town, Sept. 1993)
615. Jason Lee (3)
616. Brett Angell (2)
617. Stadio Giglio
618. David Regis
619. West Ham United (6,482, Sept. 1992)
620. An opponent tried to attack him with a hammer!

WHERE DID THEY GO?

621.	Avery Osmond	Betteshanger Colliery Welfare
622.	Chris Powell	Derby County
623.	Stuart Brace	Falmouth Town
624.	Paul Byrne	Glenavon
625.	Lee Chapman	Ipswich Town
626.	Jason Harris	Nuneaton Borough
627.	Adrian Clarke	Stevenage Borough
628.	Andy Rammell	Walsall
629.	Shane Westley	Wolverhampton Wanderers
630.	Mark Warren	Fisher Atheltic

CUP RUNS

631.	Brentford
632.	Yeovil Town
633.	Ipswich Town
634.	23
635.	Crystal Palace
636.	Torquay United
637.	Bristol Rovers
638.	Colchester United
639.	Dover
640.	Peterborough United

POSITIONS IN THE LEAGUE

641.	1921/22 and 1934/35
642.	1921/22, 1996/97 and 1997/98
643.	2nd
644.	1991/92 (12th in the old Division Two)
645.	3rd (1931/32)
646.	3rd
647.	17th
648.	6th
649.	1980/81 and 2005/06
650.	2004/05

TOP LEAGUE GOALSCORERS IN A SEASON

651.	1990/91	Brett Angell (26)
652.	2005/06	Freddy Eastwood (25)
653.	1982/83	Steve Phillips (17)
654.	1993/94	Ricky Otto (15)

655.	1968/69	Billy Best (31)
656.	2003/04	Leon Constantine (25)
657.	1963/64	Micky Beesley (13)
658.	1988/89	David Crown (29)
659.	1949/50	Albert Wakefield (28)
660.	1932/33	Jack Moffitt (21)

SANDY ANDERSON

661.	Defender (fullback)
662.	1930
663.	8
664.	Folkestone Town
665.	452
666.	Nottingham Forest
667.	Harry Warren
668.	Swindon Town
669.	Most League appearances: 452
670.	Ted Fenton

ALAN LITTLE

671.	1955
672.	Midfielder
673.	1974
674.	Arthur Rowley
675.	£10,000
676.	Barnsley
677.	1999
678.	12
679.	York City
680.	Brian Little

DIVISION 4 RUNNERS-UP 1978

681.	Dave Smith
682.	Colin Morris
683.	Colin Morris
684.	Derrick Parker
685.	Watford
686.	Swansea City (3rd), Brentford (4th)
687.	25
688.	Crewe (1-0), Scunthorpe United (2-0), Halifax Town (5-0) and York City (2-1)

689.   Newport County
690.   Neil Townsend and Derrick Parker

LDV VANS TROPHY RUNNERS-UP 2005

691.   Steve Tilson
692.   Tes Bramble
693.   Shrewsbury Town
694.   Freddy Eastwood
695.   Northampton Town
696.   Swindon Town
697.   Wayne Gray and Freddy Eastwood
698.   4-3: 2-1 and 2-2
699.   Wrexham
700.   The Millennium Stadium

SOUTHEND IN THE ASSOCIATE MEMBERS' CLUB

701.   Leyton Orient, Gillingham and Wimbledon
702.   Colchester United, Leyton Orient and Watford
703.   5-0 and the programme announced the dismissal of manager Peter Morris and coach Colin Harper, with Bobby Moore taking temporary charge
704.   He stopped Rovers' Aiden McCaffery from choking on his tongue
705.   John Gymer
706.   Cambridge United and Fulham
707.   Sherpa Van Trophy
708.   Leo Roget
709.   They all came in the second half of the match
710.   Brett Angell, Steve Tilson and Andy Ansah

LOAN PLAYERS

711.   Charlie Williamson
712.   Grimsby Town and AFC Bournemouth
713.   Andy Turner
714.   Ian Selley
715.   Lee Chapman
716.   Darren Blewitt
717.   Brian Barry-Murphy
718.   Paul Harding
719.   Brighton and Hove Albion
720.   Adem Poric

UNUSUAL SOURCES

721.	Greig Shepherd	Eastern Athletic
722.	Buck Fryar	Shoebury Town
723.	Andy Thomson	Queen of the South
724.	Sandy Anderson	Newburgh Juniors
725.	Graham Franklin	Lowestoft Town
726.	David Cunningham	Brechin City
727.	Jimmy Clark	Benburb Star
728.	Nathan Jones	CD Numancia
729.	Joe Hall	Backworth Percy
730.	Scott Forbes	Saffron Walden Town

KEVIN MAHER

731. Ilford
732. 1998 (January)
733. True
734. Alvin Martin
735. Burnley
736. 1998/99 and 2001/02
737. 2000/01 & 2006/07
738. Rob Newman
739. 14
740. 2004/05 and 2005/06

TOTAL APPEARANCES FOR SOUTHEND UNITED

741.	Harry Threadgold	343
742.	Tony Hadley	342
743.	Tony Bentley	419
744.	Chris Powell	290
745.	Paul Clark	358
746.	Alan Moody	507
747.	Billy Moore	304
748.	Sandy Anderson	483
749.	Paul Sansome	357
750.	Ronnie Pountney	401

ANDY SMILLIE

751. 1941
752. 1964
753. Ted Fenton
754. 29

755. Shrewsbury Town
756. Watford
757. Scunthorpe United
758. Workington
759. 180
760. Luton Town

JOHN McKINVEN
761. Midfielder/Winger
762. 1960
763. Raith Rovers
764. Scottish
765. 62
766. Brentford
767. Northampton Town
768. Andy Smillie
769. Bobby Gilfillan
770. Broken leg

BILL GARNER
771. 1947
772. Centre forward
773. English
774. Bedford Town
775. True
776. 1969
777. Geoff Hudson
778. 41
779. 102
780. Chelsea

RON POUNTNEY
781. 1955
782. 26
783. Chelmsford City
784. Arthur Rowley
785. Midfielder
786. True
787. Charlton Athletic
788. Blackpool
789. Arthur Rowley, Dave Smith, Peter Morris and Bobby Moore

790.   *£3,000*

RICHARD CADETTE

791.   *True*
792.   *Centre forward*
793.   *49*
794.   *1985*
795.   *Leyton Orient*
796.   *Leyton Orient*
797.   *Bobby Moore*
798.   *Rochdale*
799.   *FA Cup (second round)*
800.   *Sheffield United*

OTHER BOOKS BY PETER MILES:

Non-League Grounds of Essex & East London
ISBN: 1-900257-01-9
Price: £5.95

Non-League Grounds of Hertfordshire
ISBN: 1-900257-04-1   978-1900257-04-6
Price: £5.95

Football in Ireland
ISBN: 0-953661-90-3   978-0953661-90-9
Price: £5.99

Potted Shrimps
ISBN: 1-874427-23-2   978-1-874427-23-0
Price: £10.95

Images of Sport: Southend United
ISBN: 0-752420-89-5   978-0752420-89-9
Price: £10.99

Southend United: 100 Greats
ISBN: 0-752421-77-8   978-0752421-77-3
Price: £12.00

Homes of Non-League Football
ISBN: 0-752427-23-7   978-0752427-23-2
Price: £9.99

Southend United: 50 Classic Matches
ISBN: 0-752430-72-6   978-0-752430-72-0
Price: £10.99

OTHER BOOKS BY CHRIS COWLIN:

The Official Norwich City Football Club Quiz Book

Foreword by: Bryan Gunn

ISBN: 1-904444-80-6   978-1-904444-80-0

Price: £8.99

Will you be singing like a Canary as you fly with ease through this book's 1,000 challenging quiz questions about Norwich City Football Club, or will you have flown the Nest too soon and come crashing to the ground spitting feathers?

Covering all aspects of the club's history, including top goalscorers, transfers, managers, Cup competitions, League positions, awards, legendary players and nationalities, it will push to the limit even the most ardent aficionados' knowledge of their favourite team.

With a fitting foreword by the legendary Bryan Gunn, this book is guaranteed to trigger fond recollections of all the nail-biting matches and colourful characters that have shaped the club over the years, as well as providing a wealth of interesting facts and figures with which to impress your friends and family.

The Official Colchester United Quiz Book

Foreword by: Karl Duguid

ISBN: 1-904444-88-1   978-1-904444-88-6

Price: £5.99

Question: How many U's are there in Colchester? Answer: One, of course - as all Colchester United fans ought to know. And, if that little teaser caught you out, then brace yourselves for 700 more tricky questions, relating to your favourite team, the U's.

Covering all aspects of the club, from players and managers to nationalities and every conceivable tournament, you will be required to U's your brainpower to its limit to come up with all the answers and amaze (or otherwise) your friends and family with the depth of your knowledge about the club.

With a fitting Foreword by Karl Duguid, this book will trigger recollections of favourite players past and present, nail-biting matches, and all the club's highs and lows over their long history. A veritable treasure trove of facts and figures is at your fingertips – enjoy!

OTHER BOOKS BY CHRIS COWLIN:

The West Ham United Quiz Book
Foreword by: Julian Dicks
ISBN: 1-904444-99-7   978-1-904444-99-2
Price: £6.99

Now is the time to find out how much you West Ham United fans really know, but be warned – your brains are sure to take a hammering as you struggle to answer the 1,000 challenging questions in this quiz book, covering every aspect of the team's history, such as players, managers, opponents, scores, transfers, nationalities and every competition you can think of.

You'll be arguing with the referee and pleading for extra time as the questions spark recollections and ardent discussions of the legendary greats and nail-biting matches that have shaped the club over the years.

With a fitting foreword by Hammers legend Julian Dicks, and bulging with important facts and figures, this book will entertain as well as educate, but be prepared for a few fouls and yellow cards along the way.

The Gooners Quiz Book
Foreword by: Bob Wilson
ISBN: 1-904444-77-6   978-1-904444-77-0
Price: £8.99

Will you do the Gooners proud as you display an impressive knowledge of your favourite club, Arsenal, or will you instead prove yourself to be a complete goon, as trip over your own feet in search of the answers to the 1,000 cunning questions in this quiz book?

Covering every aspect of the club's history from players to managers and from national to international competitions since its foundation over a century ago, and with a fitting Foreword by former Scotland and Arsenal goalkeeping legend and TV presenter, Bob Wilson, this book will challenge Gooners fans of all ages as well as providing fascinating facts and figures both to enthral and to trigger fond memories and ardent discussions.

If you find yourself floundering, you can recover your dignity and find consolation in the fact that £1 from the sale of every book will go to the Willow Foundation, a charity founded by Bob and Megs Wilson and dedicated to arranging individually tailored 'Special Days' for seriously ill young adults.

OTHER BOOKS BY CHRIS COWLIN:

Celebrities' Favourite Football Teams
Foreword by: Sir Alex Ferguson CBE
ISBN: 1-904444-84-9   978-1904444-84-8
Price: £6.99

We all like to delve into the minds and lives of our beloved celebrity figures, but this fascinating read is not celebrity gossip, it comes straight from the horse's mouth to reveal all you ever wanted to know about celebrities' favourite football teams and players.

With a fitting Foreword by footballing legend Sir Alex Ferguson CBE, this book is a must-read for football fans who wish to know which celebrity is a fellow aficionado of their club, or perhaps a supporter of 'the enemy', as well as for the rest of the population, who just love to know what makes our celebrities tick.

And it is also a must-buy, as all royalties from the sale of this book will be donated to The Willow Foundation, a charity set up by the legendary Bob Wilson and his wife Megs in 1999 to enable seriously ill young adults to enjoy the treat of a 'Special Day' with family and friends.

The Official Watford Football Club Quiz Book
Foreword by: Graham Taylor OBE
ISBN: 1-904444-85-7   978-1-904444-85-5
Price: £7.99

Be prepared to stir up a veritable hornets nest as you strive to meet the challenge of answering 1,000 testing questions about Watford Football Club. This quiz book certainly has the 'ouch' factor, guaranteeing that even the most ardent fan will get stung several times along the way.

Covering every subject imaginable about the Hornets, from players of old to the most recent Cup competitions, it not only contains a wealth of interesting facts and figures but also will stir up fond memories of all the great personalities and nail-biting matches that have helped to mould the Club throughout its long history.

With a fitting Foreword by legendary Watford Manager, Graham Taylor OBE, this book will provide hours of entertainment for the whole family who, whilst licking their wounds, can console themselves in the knowledge that £1 from the sale of each copy will be donated to the charity Sense, which helps deaf and blind people of all ages lead fuller and happier lives.

REVIEWS

"Many interesting and diverse questions covering all aspects of Southend United, and to suit all abilities."
- Dave Goody, Author of 'Southend United' and 'Southend United A-Z'

"How well do you know the boys from Roots Hall? From Chris Powell to Brett Angell, The Southend United Quiz Book will test the knowledge of the biggest Shrimper!"
- www.4thegame.com

"This book covers all aspects of the club, from the players to the history of the club. It will provide a great fun and a challenge for even the most loyal Southend United fan."
- www.southendunited-mad.co.uk

"The highs and lows of the Shrimpers are captured between the pages of 'The Southend United Quiz Book'. 800 questions to tax the knowledge of even the most ardent Blues fan. This book's a real winner!"
- www.sarfend.co.uk

"A very interesting book. I thought I knew a bit about Southend United! A must for all Southend supporters."
- Dean Austin

"Have as much fun with this book as I did with the Shrimpers!"
- Freddy Eastwood

"This book brought back so many great memories of the club. A true gem - every Southend fan will enjoy this book."
- Peter Taylor

"You often see the phrase 'a must for any self respecting supporter' but this time the phrase is well placed as this book is a MUST!"
- Geoffrey King